Apache Warriors

Other books in the Daily Life series:

DAILY LIFE

Apache Warriors

Patricia D. Netzley

KIDHAVEN
PRESS™

THOMSON

———— ✦ ————™

GALE

San Diego • Detroit • New York • San Francisco • Cleveland
New Haven, Conn. • Waterville, Maine • London • Munich

© 2003 by KidHaven Press. KidHaven Press is an imprint of The Gale Group, Inc.,
a division of Thomson Learning, Inc.

KidHaven™ and Thomson Learning™ are trademarks used herein under license.

For more information, contact
KidHaven Press
27500 Drake Rd.
Farmington Hills, MI 48331-3535
Or you can visit our Internet site at http://www.gale.com

LIBRARY OF CONGRESS CATALOGING-IN-PUBLICATION DATA

Netzley, Patricia D.
  Apache warriors / by Patricia D. Netzley.
    p. cm.—(Daily life)
  Includes bibliographical references.
  Summary: Based partly on excerpts from the autobiography of Geronimo,
  describes life as an Apache, growing up with Apache values, rituals to become
  a warrior, and the obligations and rules of conduct in war.
  ISBN 0-7377-0989-8 (hardback : alk. paper)
  1. Apache Indians—Juvenile literature. 2. Apache Indians—Warfare—Juvenile
  literature. [1. Apache Indians. 2. Indians of North America—New Mexico.] I. Title.
  II. Series.
    E99 .A6 N47 2003
    979.004'972—dc21

2001006813

Printed in China

Contents

CHAPTER ONE

Growing Up Apache

The Apache Indians lived throughout the American Southwest between the 1300s and the 1880s. By the mid–nineteenth century between ten thousand and twenty-five thousand Apache lived in the regions of Arizona, New Mexico, parts of Texas, and northern Mexico. They were divided into several small groups called subtribes, each of which shared a geographical area within Apache lands. The most important of these subtribes were the Chiricahua, the Mescalero, the Lipan, the Jicarilla, the Mimbreno, and the Coyotera.

Members of each of these subtribes lived together in communities called bands. Each band consisted of several extended families, or clans, that pooled their food and other resources. Apache bands varied widely in size depending on how much food was available in their territory and how many people were necessary to protect the band's resources from theft by outsiders. Some bands had only a few people, while others had dozens or even hundreds. In addition, someone from one band might decide to live with another band. Such decisions were usually made when all of a subtribe's bands came to-gether at a prearranged site to trade and socialize. This type of event happened at least once a year, at times when the weather was good.

Teepees

Except during the winter snows, most Apache bands were nomadic, which means that they did not live in per-manent villages but instead moved their villages from place to place. They did this because their main source of food was the buffalo. The carcass of this migrating ani-mal was too large to be carried long distances, so Apache villages had to be close to wherever the buffalo had been

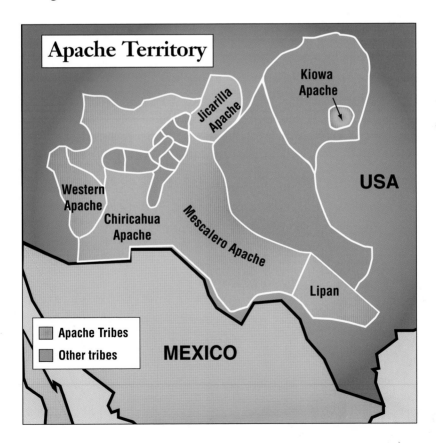

Apache Territory

Kiowa Apache

Jicarilla Apache

Western Apache

Chiricahua Apache

Mescalero Apache

USA

Lipan

Apache Tribes

Other tribes

MEXICO

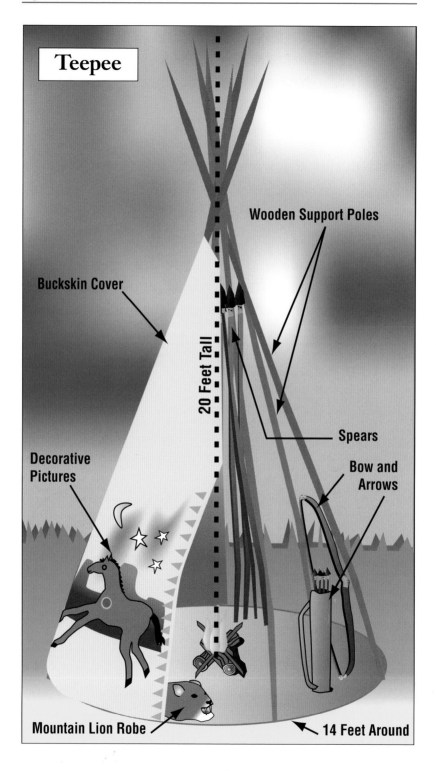

Teepee

Wooden Support Poles

Buckskin Cover

20 Feet Tall

Spears

Decorative
Pictures

Bow and
Arrows

Mountain Lion Robe

14 Feet Around

killed. Therefore, Apache homes, called teepees (some-times spelled *tepees* or *tipis*) were designed to be easily taken apart, moved, and rebuilt.

Made of wooden poles covered with animal hides, the typical teepee was a cone-shaped tent about twenty feet tall and fourteen feet in diameter, big enough for five to eight people. In his autobiography, the Apache warrior Geronimo described his own teepee:

> The tepee was made of buffalo hides and in it were many bear robes, lion hides, and other trophies of the chase, as well as my spears, bows, and arrows. Alope [Geronimo's wife] had made many little decorations of beads and drawn work on buck-skin, which she placed in our tepee. She also drew many pictures on the walls of our home.[1]

Raiding

The Apache moved their teepees several times a year, not only so they could follow game animals but also so they could escape enemies. The Apache had many enemies. Prior to the seventeenth century, they were often at war with other tribes of Native Americans. During the sev-enteenth, eighteenth, and nineteenth centuries, the Apache were at war with a succession of Spanish, Mexi-can, and American soldiers and settlers who moved onto Apache lands.

These people usually became involved in wars with the Apache because of the Apache practice of raiding. When-ever an Apache band ran low on supplies, its men—also

An Apache raiding party attacks a neighboring tribe.

called braves or warriors—would sneak into other tribes' settlements to raid, or take, their supplies. If any member of the Apache raiding party was killed during this thievery, then the Apache would declare war on everyone who lived in the settlement they had raided. No one knows how many Native Americans the Apache killed as a result of this practice. However, between 1821 and 1836 they killed more than five thousand Mexican settlers because of raid-related wars.

Learning the Ways of the Warrior

The Apache were a deadly enemy because they were taught from an early age to be extremely skilled at warfare. Apache boys were brought up to believe that it was important to prove oneself in battle, and from the age of seven they were taught to be skilled warriors. They learned to ride horses bareback and practiced with bows and arrows, first on small prey and later on bigger game. For example, Geronimo explained:

> There were many rabbits in our range, and we also hunted them on horseback. Our horses were trained to follow the rabbit at full speed, and as they approached them we would swing from one side of the horse and strike the rabbit with our hunting club. If he was too far away we would throw the stick and kill him. This was great sport when we were boys, but as warriors we seldom hunted small game.[2]

Geronimo also recalled playing games in which he pretended to be a warrior:

> With my brothers and sisters I played about my father's home. Sometimes we played at hide-and-seek. . . . Sometimes we played that we were warriors. We would practice stealing upon some object that represented an enemy, and in our childish imitation often perform the feats of war.[3]

Apache boys were also given many tasks to make them more physically fit. These tasks included running up mountains and swimming in icy streams. Sometimes a boy was ordered to run several miles while keeping water in his mouth without swallowing it in order to learn physical and mental discipline. Boys also participated in wrestling, fighting, and contests with slingshots or bows and arrows.

Warrior Training

Many Apache games involved throwing things at targets to help improve a boy's aim. One of the most popular games was hoop and pole, which required players to throw a pole through a rolling hoop and knock it down. Only males were allowed to play this game. In fact, women were not even allowed to watch it, because the players thought it would bring bad luck.

In addition to playing games, Apache boys listened to their elders lecture on how a warrior should behave. Historian Frederick Turner, in an introduction to Geronimo's autobiography, tells of an Apache warrior who told Turner that as soon as he was old enough to understand, "I was told who were our enemies."[4] Turner also quotes a warrior who told a boy under his teaching:

> My son, you know no one will help you in this world. You must do something. You run to that mountain and come back. This will make you strong. My son, you know no one is your friend, not even your sister, your father, or your mother. Your legs are your friends; your brain is your

friend; your eyesight is your friend; your hair is your friend; your hands are your friends; you must do something with them. . . . If you go somewhere, you must beat the enemy who are attacking you before they get over the hill. . . . Before they beat you, you must get in front of them . . . and bring them back dead. Then all the people will be proud of you. Then you will be the only man. Then all the people will talk about you. That is why I talk to you in this way.[5]

Two young Native American men compete at hoop and pole, a game that helps improve aim.

A novice warrior stands before his family while a brave holds the scalp of the novice's victim.

When he reached the age of fifteen, an Apache boy would formally announce to the other males in his family that he had learned his childhood lessons well and was ready to become a beginning, or novice, warrior. At this point he would set aside his boyhood games and train more seriously for the role he would take on as a man. However, because of his early training, he was already skilled at warfare, and his novice period usually passed easily.

Becoming a Warrior

No young man could become a warrior without proving his worth to the men of his band. An Apache did not want to fight beside someone who was unskilled or untrustworthy. Therefore, a novice accompanied warriors on a total of four raids and/or battles before he could become a warrior himself, watching and learning from experienced fighters.

The Tools of the Novice

Before going on his first raid, the novice had to recite various rules followed by the warriors of his band. Different bands had different rules, but all of the rules had the same purpose: to keep the Apache from getting captured by an enemy. Therefore, they included rules such as: "You should travel only at night," and "You must never go to a waterhole during the day."[6]

Once the novice proved that he knew the rules, he was given the three tools of a novice: a novice cap, a scratching stick, and a drinking tube. These items did not belong to the novice. They were merely used by him until he

A warrior explains the battle strategy to novices who will accompany the party on their raid.

became a warrior, whereupon they were passed on to a new novice. The new warrior then received warrior versions of the same items.

The novice cap was a war hat adorned with bird feathers. However, these feathers were more than just decorations. The Apache thought that the feathers of certain birds could provide novices with the traits they needed to become good warriors. To this end, most novice caps were adorned with oriole feathers for clear thinking, hummingbird feathers for speed, quail feathers for stealth, and eagle down for protection.

The scratching stick was used to scratch an itch. The Apache believed that anyone going off to meet an enemy without a scratching stick would get hard, scaly skin. Likewise, they believed that anyone taking part in a raid or war party who drank water without sucking it through a drinking tube (a hollow reed) would grow a long, tangled beard. No Apache man wanted any beard at all, or even a mustache. He believed that anyone who let his facial hair grow would become ill-tempered. Because of this belief, the Apache spent a lot of time plucking out such hairs, and they made sure they used their drinking tubes while on raids.

Proper Behavior

The novice taking part in a raid or war party also had to obey certain rules and speak in certain ways. Some of these rules were based on superstitions. For example, members of a war or raiding party were forbidden from looking back toward home after leaving to meet an enemy, because the Apache believed this would bring the

Apache were accomplished horsemen and valued their horses for travel and food.

Novice Tools

Woven Turban: With golden eagle feathers and bald eagle feathers.

Drinking Tube: Made from a hollow reed.

Scratching Stick: Prevents hard, scaly skin.

Shirt and leggings made of deer hide.

entire party bad luck. Similarly, the Apache believed that if a man ate his food warm instead of cold while on a raid, his horse would become difficult.

Other rules for members of a war or raiding party related to practical matters. For example, on the way to raid an enemy village, novice warriors had to ride at the head of the party at all times, so that it was impossible for them to fall behind and get lost. When the group camped for the night, the novices had to tend to the warriors' horses, gather firewood, cook the meals, and serve the warriors, but the novice was not allowed to eat the same food as the other warriors. According to Geronimo:

> On the first trip he [the novice] will be given only very inferior food. With this he must be contented without murmuring. On none of the four trips [required of a novice] is he allowed to select his food as the warriors do, but must eat such food as he is permitted to have.[7]

The novice was also not allowed to speak freely. Geronimo said that the novice "does whatever duties he should do without being told. He knows what things are to be done, and without waiting to be told is to do them. He is not allowed to speak to any warrior except in answer to questions or when told to speak."[8]

When speaking to the warriors, the novice had to show great respect. His words also had to be chosen in accordance with the Apache custom to use a special language while going to meet an enemy. According to

Geronimo: "After the tribe enters upon the warpath no common names are used in referring to war in any way. War is a solemn religious matter."[9] As an example, Apache warriors on a raid would say "missiles of death" instead of "arrows" and "Child of the Water" instead of "novice warrior."[10]

Staying Out of Danger

Another important rule for novices was that they were not to put themselves in any danger while in an enemy

An Apache war party rides in a single line with novices at the front.

camp. This meant that they could not actually confront an enemy during a raid. Instead, they were required to stay behind the warriors and watch their deeds to learn what to do upon becoming a warrior themselves. If a novice disobeyed this rule and was killed during a raid, it brought great shame upon the warrior leading the outing.

Warriors were also supposed to make sure that novices understood the importance of secrecy when going on a raid. Apache always sneaked up on enemy camps in darkness, raiding them in the early morning hours when their occupants were sleeping. Apache raiding parties usually had five to six men, but sometimes had as many as ten to fifteen. When they attacked, they

In the early morning an Apache raiding party scouts an enemy village.

did not destroy their enemies' homes and did not hurt anyone unless it was necessary for their own safety. By leaving the enemy unharmed, the Apache were ensuring that the same enemy camp could be raided again and again in the future.

After a successful raid, the Apache would return home as quickly as possible. Speed was extremely important to them, even if no one was chasing them. Some tribes would take a moment after a successful raid to make marks in the dirt with an arrowhead. These marks were believed to have a magical power that kept the enemy from catching the raiding party.

Being Named a Warrior

Once the novice warrior had taken part in his required four outings, he was eligible to become a warrior. However, not all novices were deemed worthy to become warriors. Geronimo explains:

> If, after four expeditions, all the warriors are satisfied that the youth has been industrious, has not spoken out of order, has been discreet in all things, has shown courage in battle, has borne all hardships uncomplainingly, and has exhibited no color of cowardice, or weakness of any kind, he may by vote of the council [of the band's warriors] be admitted as a warrior; but if any warrior objects to him upon any account he will be subjected to further tests, and if he meets these courageously, his name may again be proposed. When he has proven beyond question that he can bear

Chiricahua Apache chief Geronimo kneels with his rifle.

hardships without complaint, and that he is a stranger to fear, he is admitted to the council of the warriors in the lowest rank.[11]

Once made a warrior, the young man was allowed to join in council decisions. His rank on the council of warriors would increase over time as he became more experienced in raids and battles. As part of his council duties, an Apache warrior would vote on whether the tribe would go to war. He might also participate in trials and set punishments for wrongdoers. Eventually he might become chief, leading his council and his people in all affairs.

CHAPTER THREE

A Warrior's Days

A pache warriors were always ready for war. They also had duties and responsibilities within their bands and within their families. Family life was very important to the Apache.

Marriage

One of the first acts a young man took upon becoming a warrior was to start his own family. After selecting a wife from among the maidens of his village, the warrior would send an elder male relative—usually a father or uncle—to talk to the maiden's parents. If the girl's parents were agreeable to the match, the young man would send the parents a gift (usually ponies), and the couple was considered married. There was no wedding ceremony, although sometimes a feast was held in the couple's honor.

The newlyweds' teepee was set up right beside the teepee of the wife's family. As long as his wife's parents were alive, the young man had to show them great respect and help them with various tasks whenever they asked. The young couple also ate meals with the woman's family.

An artist's depiction of an Apache couple with their two children.

Food Preferences

The Apache ate only one meal each day, a dinner of vegetables, berries, and meat boiled together in a pot. Sometimes the meat was cooked separately on a stick. Apache warriors liked fatty meat because they believed it gave them strength. Throughout the day they chewed on pieces of dried meat into which strips of fat had been pounded. Their preferred game was deer, buffalo, antelope, and elk, but they ate other animals as well.

The Apache did not eat fish, bear, coyote, or dog, though, because they believed that all of these animals caused illness. The Apache also believed that bears were the spirits of evil people being punished for their deeds. Apache sometimes killed bears as an act of mercy, but they believed that touching the animals or their droppings, or even going near their dens, could bring insanity or bad luck.

In addition to meat, the Apache ate a great deal of nuts, berries, and fruit. As for vegetables, farming tribes planted and ate corn, beans, and squash, while other tribes relied entirely on wild plants such as onions and yucca. The acorn was a favorite food of all Apache. Once a year, as many as fifty bands from the same tribe would meet at a place rich with acorns and other food that they could store for the winter. They would stay together for several days to gather this food, and during the evenings they would play games and gamble.

Weapons

Apache warriors went on many outings to hunt for game, particularly when there were no enemies nearby to raid, because their main duty was to provide their band with food. Hunters might travel for days in search of deer and buffalo, either on horseback or on foot. They wore the same clothes on these outings as they did on every other day: a **buckskin** shirt, a breechcloth held by a **rawhide** or buckskin belt, and animal-skin shoes called moccasins. The breechcloth was a wide piece of buckskin that was tucked under the front of the man's belt, then went between the legs and was tucked over the back of the man's belt, so that its ends hung down in front and back.

Every warrior carried a knife in a rawhide or buckskin case attached to his belt. The Apache usually made the blades themselves out of stone or bone, but during

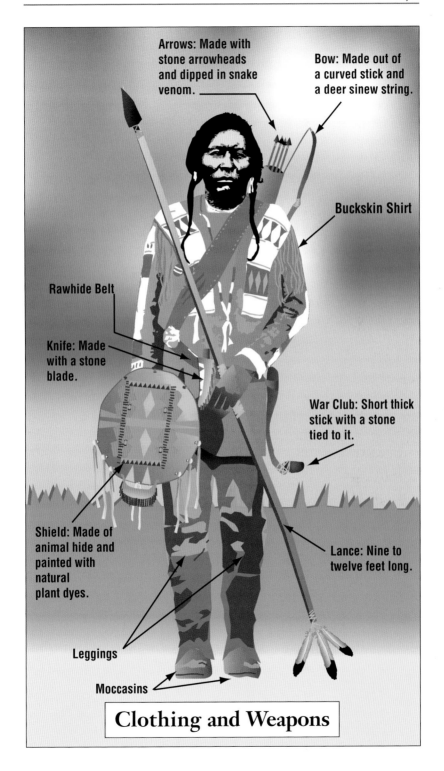

Arrows: Made with stone arrowheads and dipped in snake venom.

Bow: Made out of a curved stick and a deer sinew string.

Buckskin Shirt

Rawhide Belt

Knife: Made with a stone blade.

War Club: Short thick stick with a stone tied to it.

Shield: Made of animal hide and painted with natural plant dyes.

Lance: Nine to twelve feet long.

Leggings

Moccasins

Clothing and Weapons

raids or warfare they sometimes took metal blades from Mexicans or Americans. Every Apache warrior also carried a bow and arrow while hunting, usually strapped on his back in a case made of animal hide such as mountain lion skin. Stone or wooden arrowheads were sometimes dipped in the juice of a poisonous plant or venom of an insect. Bows were curved and had a string of deer **sinew**.

When going to war, warriors took along a war club, which was a short, thick stick. At the end of this stick was a stone wrapped in deerskin and tied to the stick with sinew. Another war weapon was the lance, which was a stick or strong plant stalk nine to twelve feet long. A few warriors also carried a shield made of animal hide and decorated with feathers. In the mid-1800s many Apache started carrying guns stolen from Mexicans and Americans as well. Because the Apache were highly skilled riders and had good aim, they easily learned to shoot expertly while on horseback.

The Di-Yin

Although the Apache made most of their own weapons, they usually had their shields made by one of their band's di-yin, also known as a **shaman** or medicine man. A di-yin was believed to have received supernatural powers from a particular being in the spirit world. These powers enabled him to cure illnesses, predict the future, change the weather, find lost objects, or bring luck in hunting, gambling, warfare, or romance.

A di-yin specialized in certain skills and rituals. Di-yins specializing in warfare not only made shields but also went with warriors into battle, so that the night before an attack they could predict where the enemy would be and perform ceremonies to increase the warriors' strength.

Sometimes an Apache warrior would try to perform magic himself, usually in order to make his environment more favorable for raids, battles, or hunting. Historian James Haley quotes one warrior who gave examples of such magic:

> If everything is dry and you want it to rain, kill a lizard or snake and turn him belly up. Or wait for a still night, one when there is no wind at all, and light a big fire, so the smoke will go up high without blowing around. . . . When you see a ring

Before battle, a shaman calls on powers from the spirit world to guide the tribe's warriors.

around the moon you know it will rain soon. If it has been raining too much and you want it to stop, the best thing is to draw a circle with charcoal around your backside, then show your [bare bottom] to the clouds. That should stop it right there. Also, catch some mice and bind them with sinew to a rock.[12]

Dreams

The Apache also believed in the power of dreams to predict the future. Dreams of certain kinds of fruit were said to foretell good fortune. Dreams of losing teeth, being caught in a flood, or being chased by animals were said to foretell misfortune. A dream of fire was supposed to be unlucky as well, but the bad luck could be dispelled by getting up immediately after the dream and lighting a fire.

The worst dreams featured people who were dead. If an Apache warrior dreamed of being offered food by someone who had died—particularly a relative—then he knew that his own death was sure to come soon. However, if he dreamed of his own death, the warrior knew he would not die. Dreams about the self were believed to predict the opposite of what was featured in the dream. In other words, if a warrior dreamed he was sick then he knew he would remain healthy, but if he dreamed he was healthy then he knew he would become sick. A warrior's worst nightmare was to dream such a prediction prior to a battle.

CHAPTER FOUR

Going to War

Apache raids on enemy camps were treated as an ordinary part of daily life. No special ceremonies or dances were held prior to a raid, and the main goal of the raiders was to sneak into an enemy camp and steal supplies without being seen. In contrast, when an Apache went to war he was seeking to prove his bravery through face-to-face confrontations with his enemy. These occasions were associated with a variety of religious rituals and special customs and clothing.

Reasons for War

Before going to war, a council of all the warriors of a band or a group of bands had to vote to fight. The most common reason for war was to avenge the death of an Apache warrior killed during a raid. During the mid-1800s, however, most Apache wars were against Americans who had attacked Apache camps.

War parties against rival tribes could involve every warrior in a band. Wars against Mexicans or Americans sometimes involved hundreds of Apache warriors from

An Apache chief stands before a council of
warriors and makes a case for war.

several bands. In addition, because Mexicans and Americans did not hesitate to attack women and children left
behind in an Apache camp, the Apache would often bring
their families along on such wars. The war party camped

some distance from the enemy, and warriors took turns protecting this camp while others rode into battle.

Special Clothing

Before going to war, Apache warriors usually put on special clothing. What they wore depended on their subtribe. For example, the Mescalero Apache wore turbans of animal fur decorated with amulets, which were magic charms believed to protect the wearer from harm. Along with these amulets the Mescalero wore red, brown, or yellow war shirts painted with symbols associated with war, such as stars and crescent moons, and decorated with fringe. The Jicarilla wore feathered headdresses instead of turbans, while the Chiricahua wore war caps decorated with eagle feathers, beads, and painted symbols.

A painting depicts a Jicarilla Apache in a feathered headdress and chest armor made of bone.

Many warriors also carried amulets into battle, perhaps inside a pouch filled with pollen from various plants that they thought would give them extra strength. This bag was tied to a cord called an izze-kloth, or Killer of Enemies, which was wrapped around the warrior's body from right shoulder to left hip. Braided from four strands of hide, the izze-kloth was made by a di-yin specializing in war. The di-yin worked magic to give the cord the power to protect the warrior from danger. To call down this power, the warrior chanted certain words, but some believed that if he used the chant too often, the cord would lose its magic.

Warriors sometimes had a di-yin paint their faces prior to battle, believing it would bring them luck. Warriors from different bands used different traditional patterns and colors of paint. For example, eastern Chiricahuas wore a red stripe down their noses, while western Chiricahuas painted their faces with white dots.

The War Dance

Just before leaving for battle, the warriors attended a ceremony called a war dance or angry dance. Held around a fire, it began with four warriors dancing certain steps around the flames to the beat of drums. Their dance steps were usually in patterns of four, because the Apache associated the number four with powerful magic.

After the first four warriors had danced for a few minutes, others joined in until every warrior was dancing. Any warrior who did not dance was considered disgraced. Women, however, were not allowed to participate, even if they were planning to fight in the battle. (Women

Warriors take part in a ceremonial war dance.

sometimes fought when there were not enough male warriors.)

As the war dance progressed, the men's movements became wild, and they often whooped and yelled. Warriors also sometimes playacted the actions they intended to perform during the upcoming battle. Their dancing could go on for an entire night and might be repeated for four nights in a row.

Battle Tactics

Once at war, the Apache used a variety of tactics to help them succeed. They often attacked their enemy in a canyon or rocky area, where escape was difficult, and set fire to the brush to create smoke and confusion. The surprise attacks were usually done on foot because horses made too much noise. However, horses would be waiting nearby to aid their escape. In battle the Apache preferred to strike suddenly, kill as many enemies as possible, as quickly as possible, and then run away. They made sure they were very familiar with their escape route before they attacked.

To make their escape more quickly, the Apache carried few supplies with them. They were experts at finding food where most of their American enemies could not. The Apache were also so physically fit that they could travel as many as fifty miles per day on foot and several times that distance on horseback. When someone was chasing them, a group of warriors would scatter in many directions, making it more difficult for their enemies to pursue. The warriors would meet later at a prearranged place as many as one hundred miles away.

Treatment of Enemies

Sometimes the Apache took an enemy captive, particularly if the enemy refused to put up a fight. If the captive was a woman, they would usually take her back to their camp where she would live as someone's wife or slave.

Captured boys under the age of seven were adopted by warriors and raised as Apache.

Older boys and men were killed, but those who had killed an Apache were tortured first. Sometimes a warrior took as a souvenir the **scalp** of an enemy he had killed, but only if that enemy was someone whom he had considered to be a worthy opponent. These scalps were then used in a celebration called a scalp dance, which took place after the battle and was similar to a war dance. In a scalp dance, warriors placed scalps on poles and carried

An Apache warrior sets prairie brush on fire to create a smoke diversion.

Victorious Apache fighters perform the scalp dance, dangling their trophies from spears.

them around a bonfire. After the dance the warriors would destroy the scalps, because they believed that keeping them would bring bad luck.

Death

Because of their fighting skills, in most battles far fewer Apache were killed than their enemies. Sometimes, however, an Apache warrior did die, and whenever possible his body was brought back to his family for burial or **entombment**. Geronimo described the entombment of his father, who died of an illness:

When he passed away . . . they arrayed him in his best clothes, painted his face . . . wrapped a rich blanket around him, saddled his favorite horse, bore his arms in front of him, and led his horse behind, repeating in wailing tones his deeds of valor as they carried his body to a cave in the mountain. Then they slew his horses, and we gave away all of his other property, as was customary in our tribe, after which his body was deposited in the cave. . . . His grave is hidden by piles of stone.[13]

Murdering Women and Children

The Apache tried not to harm women and children during warfare. In contrast, Americans often murdered Apache women and children even during peacetime. For example, in 1871 near Camp Grant, an American military post in Arizona, U.S. soldiers attacked and brutally murdered more than 125 sleeping Apache women and children.

Faced with such an enemy, some Apache bands signed treaties with the U.S. government to end the slaughter of their families, even though their warriors were undefeated. Beginning in 1870, these Apache moved from their lands onto government-run lands called Indian reservations. By 1886, nearly all Apache lived in such places.

Once on reservations, the Apache received their food, supplies, clothes, and houses from the U.S. government. They could no longer hunt, nor could they raid their neighbors. Without freedom to move across

Faced with the slaughter of their families, a band
of Apache warriors surrender to U.S. troops.

the American Southwest, the Apache lost an important
aspect of their culture. Their way of life was forced to
end. However, the descendants of Apache warriors
continue to live today on reservations in various parts
of the United States.

Notes

Chapter One: Growing Up Apache
1. Quoted in Frederick Turner, ed., *Geronimo: His Own Story. The Autobiography of a Great Patriot Warrior, As Told to S.M. Barrett.* New York: Meridian/Penguin Books, 1996, p. 71.
2. Quoted in Turner, *Geronimo,* pp. 67–68.
3. Quoted in Turner, *Geronimo,* p. 59.
4. Quoted in Turner, *Geronimo,* p. 17.
5. Quoted in Turner, *Geronimo,* p. 18.

Chapter Two: Becoming a Warrior
6. Quoted in James L. Haley, *Apaches: A History and Culture Portrait.* Garden City, NY: Doubleday, 1981, p. 133.
7. Quoted in Turner, *Geronimo,* pp. 148–49.
8. Quoted in Turner, *Geronimo,* p. 149.
9. Quoted in Turner, *Geronimo,* p. 149.
10. Haley, *Apaches,* p. 134.
11. Quoted in Turner, *Geronimo,* p. 149.

Chapter Three: A Warrior's Days
12. Quoted in Haley, *Apaches,* p. 73.

Chapter Four: Going to War
13. Quoted in Turner, *Geronimo,* pp. 69–70.

Glossary

buckskin: A soft leather made from the hide of a deer.

entombment: The placement of a body in a tomb.

rawhide: An animal hide left untreated with tannic acid (an element in oak bark used to change hide into leather).

scalp: The skin and hair from the head of an Apache enemy killed in battle.

shaman: A priest of shamanism, a religion in which people believe they can influence supernatural beings to do good or evil on earth.

sinew: An animal tendon dried and used as string or cord.

For Further Exploration

Anne Ake, *The Apache*. San Diego: Lucent Books, 2001. This book tells about the lives of all members of Apache society.

Peter Aleshire, *Reaping the Whirlwind: The Apache Wars*. New York: Facts On File, 1998. Written by an expert on the Apache, this book for more advanced readers tells about battles between Apache warriors and American soldiers.

Gordon C. Baldwin, *The Apache Indians: Raiders of the Southwest*. New York: Four Winds Press, 1978. For more advanced readers, this book offers detailed information about the lifestyles of the Apache.

Sonia Bleeker, *The Apache Indians*. New York: William Morrow, 1975. This book gives basic information about the lifestyles and history of the Apache.

James L. Haley, *Apaches: A History and Culture Portrait*. Garden City, NY: Doubleday, 1981. For more advanced readers, this book offers in-depth information about Apache history and culture.

Candy Moulton, *Everyday Life Among the American Indians: 1800 to 1900*. Cincinnati: Writers Digest Books, 2001. This book provides basic facts about the everyday lives of the Apache, as well as many other Native American tribes living between the years 1800 and 1900.

Petra Press, *The Apache.* Minneapolis: Compass Point Books, 2001. For younger readers, this book gives basic information about the Apache.

Andrew Santella, *The Apache.* New York: Childrens Press, 2001. This book tells how the Apache lived.

George Edward Stanley, *Geronimo: Young Warrior.* New York: Aladdin Paperbacks, 2001. This book tells about Geronimo's childhood.

Frederick Turner, ed., *Geronimo: His Own Story. The Autobiography of a Great Patriot Warrior, As Told to S.M. Barrett.* New York: Meridian/Penguin Books, 1996. In this book the famous Apache warrior Geronimo tells the story of his life.

Index